W9-AKB-718

3 1489 00568 3063

DANIEL RADCLIFFE
NO ORDINARY WIZARD

BY GRACE NORWICH

Simon Spotlight
New York London Toronto Sydney

FREEPORT MEMORIAL LIBRARY

$4.99

If you purchased this book
without a cover, you should be aware that this
book is stolen property. It was reported as "unsold and destroyed"
to the publisher, and neither the author nor the publisher
has received any payment for this "stripped book."

This book is neither authorized nor endorsed by Daniel Radcliffe
or any of the production companies listed herein.

SIMON SPOTLIGHT
An imprint of Simon & Schuster
Children's Publishing Division
1230 Avenue of the Americas
New York, New York 10020

Text © 2005 by Simon & Schuster, Inc.
All rights reserved, including the right of
reproduction in whole or in part in any form.

SIMON SPOTLIGHT and colophon are registered
trademarks of Simon & Schuster, Inc.

Manufactured in the United States of America

First Edition 10 9 8 7 6 5 4

ISBN-13: 978-1-4169-1390-0
ISBN-10: 1-4169-1390-4
Library of Congress Catalog Card Number 2005929055

CONTENTS

1 DAN'S MAGIC

When the millions of Harry Potter fans out there think of the sweet, unassuming boy wizard they have grown to love, a picture of Daniel Radcliffe immediately pops into their heads. That's because Dan—as all his friends and family members call him—is the young actor who, at age eleven, won the role of Harry Potter in the first movie and has been the face of the famous wizard on-screen ever since!

So just how similar is Dan to the famous wizard we all know and love? Well, quite similar, actually. Except for his lack of magical powers, Dan shares a lot of similarities with the fictional character that has made him a household name. First off, they are both British, and very cute! But there are a lot of other, somewhat less obvious, characteristics that they share. According to Dan, they seem to have so much in common he has even joked that one day he'll have to go into therapy, because every time he reads J. K.'s books he finds more links between his and Harry's personalities. Not that the two boys share any bad traits. In fact, it's just the opposite!

"We have curiosity [and] loyalty," Dan told *People* magazine—two very important attributes to have. Despite his ever-rising celebrity status, Dan has managed to remain pretty levelheaded, and becoming famous hasn't at all changed the way he treats his friends and loved ones or lessened the time he makes for them in his life. Actually, whenever he gets a chance on the movie set, Dan keeps in touch with his school chums by telephone, e-mail, or text messaging. Just as Draco Malfoy discovered about Harry at the beginning of their first year at Hogwarts, Dan also has no trouble spotting the wrong sort of people. He knows how essential it is to keep sight of the important things in life. Instead of getting wrapped up in his fame, Dan, like Harry, keeps his head out of the clouds and devotes his time to the "right" sort of people, the friends who have always stood by him, movie star or not.

Another similarity that Dan and the fictional wizard seem to share is a level of wisdom and maturity that is beyond their years, which is probably due to the fact that they both had to handle a great deal of responsibility at such a young age. While Harry has the special lightning-bolt scar that means he will have to single-handedly battle the forces of evil and save the world, Dan has had his own earthly challenges. The Harry Potter books and movies have all been such huge hits that there is hardly a corner of the globe that hasn't been touched by the unprecedented phenomenon. Because of this, an insane media storm, usually reserved only for the top echelon of A-list celebrities such as Tom Cruise and Brad Pitt, has surrounded Dan as he has grown from a skinny, small kid to the hunky teenager he is today. Throughout his time in the spotlight, however, Dan has proved himself to be as gracious and professional as any adult.

Not that Dan, or Harry for that matter, is always a choirboy. They both partake in their fair share of mischief—just ask any of the other actors on the Harry Potter sets who have been on the receiving end of Dan's practical jokes. But they never take it too far. Although they both "get in trouble," as Dan told *People*, "we don't break the rules, we just kind of bend them."

Moviegoers watching Harry Potter escape one hair-raising adventure after another may think they know Dan Radcliffe. Sometimes it's so easy to get swept up in the magic and mania of Harry Potter that people start thinking of Dan and the fictional character he plays on-screen as one and the same. But let the record show, despite their similarities, Dan is different from the character he plays in many ways. Just as Clark Kent took off his glasses to unveil Superman, when Dan takes off his trademark Harry Potter spectacles and that snug, Hogwarts blazer, he reveals his true self. When he is not battling the forces of evil on the big screen, Dan likes to kick back and listen to music by the Sex Pistols or New York Dolls, brash loud punk music one wouldn't associate with such a soft-spoken and polite boy. And he's got a lot of other tricks up his sleeve. Let's discover the magic that has made Dan Radcliffe into one of the hottest, most talented young stars in the world.

2 NOT YOUR TYPICAL ACTOR

Daniel Jacob Radcliffe was born on July 23, 1989, in London, England, to Alan Radcliffe and Marcia Gresham. He grew up in the well-to-do neighborhood of Fulham, in the southwest part of the city. Daniel attended Sussex House, an exclusive all-boys private school in Chelsea, where his favorite classes were gym and science. Dan has always been an individual, not one to follow the crowd. At an early age he didn't associate with the in group, but rather rooted for the kind of underdog that he would later come to embody playing the character of Harry Potter.

"I've never been one of the cool people at school, but then again, I don't get the people who are cool," Dan told the Associated Press in an interview. Not one to comfortably badmouth anyone, even school snobs, he added, "It's not that I don't like them. It's just that they don't interest me."

Although Dan expressed interest in acting at a young age, he wasn't dead set on making it his profession. As a young boy Dan had many other interests, including medicine, particularly neurological disorders, and thought about pursuing a career in one of those other fields. However, despite these interests, Daniel felt that the stage was his true calling—luckily for the millions of fans who currently adore him. His very first acting experiences were in small school productions. "My earliest memory of acting was playing a monkey in a school play, when I was about six," Dan told E! Online. "I had floppy ears and orange makeup, and I had to wear tights. I think I went on and danced around for about forty seconds or something. I hope nobody ever digs up a picture of me in that, because it was embarrassing."

School plays were a beginning, but Dan learned more about the world of professional acting from a source much closer to home: his parents. His father, Alan, was a literary agent and his mother, Marcia, was a casting director. In the beginning of her career, Marcia turned her creative energy toward theater and produced some plays, until, eventually, she set up her own casting agency. Marcia forged a successful career, taking on the position of casting director on many well-known British productions, including *The Inspector Lynley Mysteries* series for television and a recent made-for-TV drama called *The Government Inspector*. Alan had also tried his hand at acting. He trained for the theater at an acting school in Guildford. But he eventually gave it up and went to work as an agent for International Creative Management, one of the world's largest talent and literary agencies.

Because of their professions and interest in the arts, the Radcliffes socialized in industry circles, rubbing elbows with high-level professionals who worked in television, theater, and film. And these people really knew the business; they could tell you exactly what would work and what wouldn't. It almost seems inevitable that one of these well-trained, seasoned professionals would discover Dan's potential. Sure enough, a family friend suggested to Alan and Marcia that Daniel would be good for the title part in a television production of *Oliver Twist*. Dan was excited at the prospect and really wanted to give it a shot, but Alan and Marcia were reluctant to allow Dan to enter the world of professional acting. Being involved in the performing arts themselves, they were aware of the pressures and sacrifices that go with being a professional child actor. They worried about Daniel missing out on a normal childhood; they feared that he might be taken advantage of or pressured into adopting a lifestyle of intense work and grueling hours at too young an age. They did not want the decision they made to be one that they would later regret. And so, the opportunity for *Oliver Twist* came and went, and Daniel remained undiscovered.

Who knows how Dan convinced his parents to say yes the next time an opportunity came around—maybe he begged for hours, or maybe he just flashed them those big blue eyes. But when they later found out that a friend of theirs, Kate Harwood, was set to produce another

Charles Dickens tale, *David Copperfield*, for the British Broadcasting Corporation (BBC), they eased their strict stance and sent Harwood a picture of Dan. Needless to say, that photo got him called in for an audition. However, while his cute, innocent face and those big baby-blues may have gotten him the audition, his good looks didn't get him the role. He had to go through five nerve-racking tryouts before he landed the part in 1999.

Dan was only ten years old at the time, and he had never even read any of Dickens's novels. Although he enjoyed hearing some of the stories that had been written by the quintessential Victorian author, Daniel was way more impressed by Pokémon, *The Simpsons*, and the Macaulay Culkin film *Home Alone*. "Now that's really funny," he told the *Boston Herald*, referring to the classic kid flick. What's even funnier is that only about a year later, Daniel would wind up working with the director of that movie!

Although Dan's part in *David Copperfield* was his first professional role, he was already working alongside some of the best actors in the business. The cast included Dame Maggie Smith as Aunt Betsey. Maggie, who would work with Dan again about a year later in the first Harry Potter film, had been in the business for over forty years. She had won awards for her work in films, television, and on Broadway, including two Oscars, one Tony Award, and an Emmy Award. The cast also included Bob Hoskins, who played Micawber. Bob Hoskins had also been in the business for more than twenty-five years, having starred in everything from Shakespeare's *Othello* to Hollywood's *Who Framed Roger Rabbit*. Now that's range! Sir Ian McKellen, who played the mean schoolmaster, Creakle, was also one of England's most renowned actors. He had appeared in over sixty films on both television and the big screen, including a lot of favorites such as *X-Men* and *The Lord of the Rings* movies. The Irish actor Ciaran McMenamin played Copperfield as a young man for the second half of the program.

It's hard to imagine how intimidating it must have been for Dan when he first walked onto the set. This BBC production, filled with veteran actors, was a far cry from his performance as a dancing monkey. Dan told the *Boston Herald* in 2000, "On the first day it was really scary. I was afraid I would do something wrong or mess up my lines." Even the director, Simon Curtis, realized how tough it must have been for young Dan. "It was kind of weird at times to be directing some of the greatest actors in the world with the newest actor in the world," Curtis told the *Boston Herald*. But Dan wasn't chosen because of his resumé, he was chosen because of his talent. It just happened to be a bonus that Dan ended up being "a perfectly delightful boy," as Curtis told the *Boston Herald*.

David Copperfield was Dickens's favorite and most auto-biographical work, written right before he died in 1870. This film version, made for the classic series *Masterpiece Theatre*, stayed faithful to Dickens's book. In the novel, young David is raised by his widowed mother, Clara, and enjoys a happy childhood. However, when his mother marries Edward Murdstone, David gets his own bona fide evil stepfather. A series of misfortunes befall poor David. He is sent off to a strict boarding school, and then learns that his mother is dying. As if that weren't bad enough, David is sent by his stepfather to work in a London sweatshop. He has to fight to get his old life back and find the remnants of his family.

David Copperfield premiered on BBC in England on Christmas Day of 2000. Although it might seem odd that they chose Christmas Day as the date for the film's television premiere, it was actually a very wise and calculated decision. In Britain, Christmas Day television-watching is as much of a tradition as is eating mince pies, and on this widely celebrated holiday, viewer ratings skyrocket. Airing *David Copperfield* on Christmas was not only an honor, but a guarantee that it would be seen in millions of homes across Britain. The film aired in America on *Masterpiece Theatre* on PBS later that same year.

Although he was the youngest and least experienced cast member, Dan's performance in the television film gained him glowing reviews from critics, who easily recognized natural talent. In the *Christian Science Monitor*, one reviewer wrote, "The real heartthrob in this piece, though, is young Radcliffe as the child Davey—who is real as rain. Those wonderful eyes and cherubic face make us feel every thorn and every joy with equal truth."

That is the kind of review that some actors wait years and years to receive, and Daniel earned it after his very first performance!

After *Copperfield*, Dan didn't rush into a full-time acting career. He returned to his regular life of going to school, playing Pokémon, and listening to music. But his innate talent for acting couldn't grow within the confines and limitations of his school plays anymore. Soon enough Dan landed another professional role, and this time the part was in a major feature film called *The Tailor of Panama*. Daniel played Mark Pendel, the son of Louisa Pendel and Harold Pendel, the tailor for whom the film is named. *The Tailor of Panama*, based on a John Le Carré novel, couldn't have been more different from Dan's previous acting gig. The thriller revolves around a British spy who is sent to Panama because he can't seem to behave himself. The spy ends up befriending the tailor and his wife, only to discover that they are linked to some of Panama's most powerful and deviant politicians and gangsters, and so, in turn, is he.

Once again, Daniel found himself working alongside

two legendary actors, Geoffrey Rush and Jamie Lee Curtis, who played his parents in the film. In 1996 Geoffrey Rush played the off-kilter piano prodigy David Helfgott in *Shine*, a role that earned the Australian actor just about every award there is, including an Oscar, a Golden Globe, a British Academy Film Award, and an Australian Film Institute Award. Jamie Lee Curtis, the daughter of two famous actors, had proved her talents in films such as *A Fish Called Wanda* and *True Lies*, for which she won a Golden Globe Award. Ironically, while on set, Jamie Lee told Dan's mom that she thought he looked a lot like the fictional character Harry Potter. . . .

Dan had demonstrated pretty quickly that he could be a success in show business, but still his parents were hesitant about him becoming a professional actor. They had seen the heartache that their friends had endured, and watched other people's discouragement firsthand in their line of work, especially Marcia, whose position as a casting director made her witness to thousands of aspiring actors' disappointments over not getting the roles they desired. The audition process is grueling and, for the majority of actors, unrewarding. Alan and Marcia wanted to shield their son from the struggling and suffering that the typical actor must overcome. The one thing that Alan and Marcia forgot to consider was the fact that Daniel had no intention of being typical.

3 HARRY POTTER MANIA

While Dan was honing his skills as a young actor, Harry Potter was rapidly becoming a worldwide phenomenon. J. K. (short for Joanne Kathleen) Rowling first imagined the character of Harry in 1990, while she was stuck on a train for four hours somewhere between Manchester and London. "Harry just strolled into my head fully formed," J. K. told Scholastic.com in an interview.

Born near Bristol, England (a few miles from a town called Dursley, which should sound familiar since it's the name of Harry Potter's muggle relatives), J. K. always had her head in far-off places and imaginary lands. She started writing stories when she was only six years old, but her road to becoming a professional writer was as topsy-turvy as one of Harry Potter's adventures.

On that fateful train where she thought up the character that would eventually inspire her world-famous series, J. K. couldn't even find a piece of paper or a pen. So she kept all the details of her newfound idea in her head until she returned home and could write them down. Luckily, she didn't forget a single thing! Inspiration came at the funniest moments for J. K. While she was flying on an airplane (travel seems to spark this woman's imagination), the names of the Hogwarts houses—Gryffindor, Ravenclaw, Slytherin, and Hufflepuff—just popped right into her head. Again she didn't have paper, so she wrote the names on the back of a barf bag!

Developing the Harry Potter series was not an easy undertaking. She wasn't a full-time writer with a fancy desk and a quiet office to help her along. J. K. was a single mom who had to make ends meet and write in the intermittent moments while her daughter, Jessica, napped. But J. K. didn't waste much time. Even while she sat in a favorite café in Edinburgh, Nicolson's, she jotted down a lot of the book on little scraps of paper. It took her six years, but finally, the first Harry Potter book was completed.

In 1997 *Harry Potter and the Philosopher's Stone* was published, and to the delight of millions of children and their parents, a universe of witches, wizards, muggles, Quidditch, Gringotts, and fantastical creatures was born. J. K.'s American editor felt that the word "philosopher" gave an incorrect impression. He felt that the title should be more suggestive of magic, and so it became known in America as *Harry Potter and the Sorcerer's Stone*. The success of J. K.'s first book was instantaneous and amazing. It spent thirty-one weeks at No. 1 on *USA Today*'s bestselling books list. With six more books already planned out inside her head, J. K. continued to bring the story of Harry Potter and his magical world to life, and readers of all ages lined up at the door, waiting with baited breath for the moment when the new Harry Potter book hit the shelves.

The second in the series—*Harry Potter and the Chamber*

of Secrets—was published in the summer of 1998, and in the fall of that year, J. K. quickly followed with a third book, *Harry Potter and the Prisoner of Azkaban*. Sales skyrocketed with each new book, all of which made it onto the *New York Times*, *USA Today*, and *Wall Street Journal* bestseller lists. In secret warehouses the books were guarded by tight security before they went on sale. The Potter tomes flew off the shelves faster than the publisher could restock them.

On July 8, 2000, the fourth book, *Harry Potter and the Goblet of Fire*, became an unheard-of publishing sensation, selling three million books in the first forty-eight hours! *Publishers Weekly* called it "the fastest-selling book in history." The fifth in the series, *Harry Potter and the Order of the Phoenix*, had an unprecedented first print run of 6.8 million copies and a second print run of an additional 1.7 million copies. The first five books in the series spent a combined fifty-seven weeks at No. 1 on the *USA Today* list. Her sixth book, *Harry Potter and the Half-Blood Prince*—which hit bookstores July 16, 2005— had the all-time-highest initial print run of 10.8 million copies, according to its U.S. publisher, Scholastic.

All you need to do is type in "Harry Potter" on the Internet to see how Harry Potter mania is sweeping the world. People visit the Harry Potter Web site chat rooms to fiercely debate over who will win the heart of Hermione—Harry or Ron—and whether or not Harry will survive at the end of the series. Kids love Harry Potter so much they are even copying his fashion sense! According to opticians in the U.K., eight- and nine-year-old kids are more willing now than they've ever been to have their eyes examined. Prior to Harry Potter, kids would stop at nothing to keep from wearing embarrassing glasses. However, today it seems that not only do they *want* to wear glasses, but, more specifically, they want to wear glasses just like Harry's!

Part of the success of the Harry Potter series is due to the fact that the books aren't *just* for kids. The story is so exciting and compelling, and the characters so real, that grown-ups find themselves equally absorbed in the Harry Potter tale. It's estimated that forty percent of Rowling's readers are adults!

With the worldwide Harry Potter mania and J. K.'s overwhelming and ever-increasing fan base, there are over 100 million copies of Harry Potter books in print in the USA, and 260 million copies distributed to more than two hundred countries in sixty-one languages worldwide, including Zulu. It was only a matter of time before Harry Potter would leap off the page and onto the big screen. And that's where it all began for Daniel.

In 1997 David Heyman, a successful English producer, picked up a copy of *Harry Potter and the Philosopher's Stone* and read the book about the famous little boy with the scar on his forehead. David, who is originally from England, had moved to Los Angeles in 1986, and successfully produced some proper Hollywood block-busters, such as *Gorillas in the Mist*, and the ultimate gangster movie, *Goodfellas*. A little over a decade later, he returned to England and founded his own production company, Heyday Films. After reading J. K. Rowling's first bestseller, he decided that it would be the launch project for his new company. But he knew from the start that in order for the books to work on-screen, any film version would have to remain faithful to J. K. Rowling's original vision.

Before any deals could be made, David had to get

J. K.'s permission to move forward with the project. Luckily, J. K. was excited about the prospect of seeing her vision come to life on-screen, and optioned the rights for *Harry Potter and the Philosopher's Stone* to him and Warner Bros. for $700,000. That may seem like a ton of money, and of course it is for a regular person, but in the movie business, $700,000 is cheap, especially for the gold mine that the Harry Potter film series would become. At the time that he bought the rights to the book, David had "absolutely no idea that the first film would even work," as he later told the *Chicago Sun-Times*. He went on to say that initially he "thought it would be some medium-budget British thing that might catch on."

Boy was he in for a big surprise.

To turn J. K.'s magical vision into a movie, David's first step was to bring on Hollywood screenwriter Steve Kloves, who had written the screenplay for *Wonder Boys*. Despite his obvious talent and abilities, some people, including Steve, were concerned with how J. K. would feel. As Steve later told the *Philadelphia Inquirer*, "I didn't want her to think I was going to be in the business of destroying her baby." Well, it just so happens that one of J. K. Rowling's favorite movies is *The Fabulous Baker Boys*, which was written and directed by Steve himself!

Once they had selected a screenwriter, they needed to find a director. David Heyman originally approached Steven Spielberg, the director of classics such as *E.T.* and *Close Encounters of the Third Kind*. Spielberg liked the project and signed on; however, he eventually dropped out to take on the movie *Artificial Intelligence: A.I.* instead. After Spielberg left the project, the British press reported many rumors that said that Spielberg didn't just bow out, but rather left after having a dispute with J. K. Rowling, who did not approve of his plan to set the film in the U.S., and perhaps make Harry an American kid. Whether these rumors were true or false, with Spielberg out, Heyman turned to Chris Columbus, director of *Home Alone* and *Mrs. Doubtfire*, who jumped at the chance to fill in. Chris had given up the hope of directing the Harry Potter movie when he'd learned Spielberg had dibs on the gig, and had signed on to direct *Spider-Man* instead. His ten-year-old daughter, Eleanor, however, was not impressed with the creepy, crawly superhero. As Chris explained to the *Philadelphia Inquirer*, when he told her about directing *Spider-Man*, Eleanor said, "It's not *Harry Potter*, is it?"

With the producer, screenwriter, and director in place, they began the massive effort of creating the magical universe that is the world of Harry Potter. Making good use of the film's $125 million budget, the amazing team of crew members began creating Hogwarts, Diagon Alley, Hagrid's hut, and everything in between. But just two short months before they were set to begin shooting the film, a vital element was still missing. They still hadn't found their Harry Potter.

4 ONE IN TEN THOUSAND

In the fall of 1999, the producer, David Heyman, and the director, Chris Columbus, began the daunting process of casting the lead part of Harry Potter. They were positive that they would have no trouble finding someone well before the first day of filming, which was scheduled to be September 29, 2000. They were searching for someone who perfectly fit J. K. Rowling's vision. "Harry had a thin face, knobby knees, black hair and bright green eyes," she wrote about the much-beloved character in the first novel. "He wore round glasses held together with a lot of Sellotape because of all the times Dudley had punched him on the nose. The only thing Harry liked about his own appearance was a very thin scar on his forehead, which was shaped like a bolt of lightning."

The call went out and more than ten thousand boys raced to get their chance to become the famous Harry Potter. It was really important to Chris that they cast an unknown person, and not a child star, to play the part. He didn't want viewers having any preconceived notions when they saw Harry Potter up on screen. "We have to find a new face," Chris told *Dateline NBC*. "They have to believe it's Harry Potter."

Studio executives, however, had their own ideas. They wanted to get a big name to take on the part of Harry Potter. They felt that getting a familiar face to play the lead character would guarantee them a hit at the box office. Haley Joel Osment, whose role in *The Sixth Sense* gained him an Oscar nomination at the tender age of 11, was the frontrunner. Chris fought the studio honchos, insisting that Harry had to be a regular kid, and on top of that, insisting that he *had* to be British. The execs were interested to see who Chris would come up with, and allowed him to continue his search for an unknown. But by July of 2000, with only three months left before filming was set to begin, not one single boy, out of all the thousands who had auditioned, was thought to be right for the part.

At this point, everyone was getting panicky. "The fear was that the film would be called *Ron Weasley and the Philosopher's Stone* because there was just no Harry," David told the *Toronto Sun* in 2001. "We were down to four or five people who we thought had some of the qualities, but not all of them." A charismatic, loveable kid was crucial to the film's success, but the schedule of this very expensive production could not be held up because of this search for the Dream Harry, who might not even exist!

They were searching for "an old soul in a child's body," David explained to the *Toronto Sun*. That task seemed so impossible that one casting director simply quit out of frustration. Other casting directors were thinking of following suit, and one turned to Chris one day exasperated, and said, "I don't know what you want." He replied by handing her a tape of none other than Dan in *David Copperfield*, which Chris had seen months before. "*This* is what I want," he told her.

Unfortunately, it wouldn't be as simple as Chris had hoped. The casting director already knew for a fact that Dan's parents weren't going to let him try out for the part. Dan's parents still had the same opinion of professional acting—and their son's involvement in it—as they'd had when he had auditioned for *David Copperfield* and *The Tailor of Panama*. They didn't want to see him get sucked into the pressure-filled profession and get hurt and discouraged. Now, with so many young actors vying for the same part, the competition for this role was much fiercer, making it much more of a risk and a long shot than the other two roles he had auditioned for. "I kind of had a tendency to get my hopes up," Dan said on the *Today* show in 2001. "They knew that there were thousands of boys going up for the part, so they didn't want me to get my hopes up and then be disappointed, so they were just protecting me."

Then fate took over. One summer evening Dan went to the theater with his parents to see *Stones in His Pockets*, a comedy about two extras on a big American movie shooting in Ireland. In the row directly in front of the Radcliffe family were two men who knew his father. And they were behaving oddly. Instead of concentrating on the play in front of them, the men kept on turning around to stare at Dan. Did he have a stain on his tie or broccoli in his teeth? What could be more interesting than the show they had bought tickets for? "I didn't know who they were," Dan told the *Christian Science Monitor* in 2001. "But my dad asked if I'd like to go to the studio and have lunch with them."

The two men turned out to be none other than David Heyman and the screenwriter, Steve Kloves. At that lunch, Dan got a glimpse of the world that millions of kids would have done anything to see. He toured the sets and got a chance to watch the crew, who were constructing the Hogwarts School of Witchcraft and Wizardry. Needless to say he had a lot of fun. Dan also had a brief interview with the film's producers and director, and impressed everyone enough to be asked to come back and audition for the role of Harry Potter.

For his audition Dan was asked to do three screen

tests, one of which was on a broomstick! One of the scenes he read was the part when Harry, Hermione, and Ron discover that Hagrid is hiding a contraband dragon's egg. "He got me to improvise about that scene," Dan told Masterpiece Theatre Online. "He kept fumbling the lines . . . to see what I would do." Most adult actors, let alone child actors, would have crumbled in that kind of situation. "I was totally scared out of my wits. It was so terrifying," Dan told E! Online. "You go in there with these really important people, and you really feel small." However, if Dan was nervous at all, he never showed it. The day after his third screen test, he got the most important phone call of his young life. Dan was in the bathtub of all places when his dad came in and told him the good news: He had landed the part! What was Dan's reaction to the news? As he told the *Christian Science Monitor*, "I was Harry Potter. I was so happy, I cried."

The first thing Dan did was call both his grandmothers, who were very excited for him. Dan was excited too, as well he should have been, and could hardly sleep at all that first night. In fact, he woke up at

2:00 a.m. and ran into his parents' room to ask them if it was all just a big, happy dream. No, they said, it's real. And then told him to go back to bed. It was pretty late, after all.

Apparently the executives who had originally wanted a big name were just as convinced of Daniel's potential as Chris was, and on August 21, 2000, Warner Bros. formally announced that the eleven-year-old English actor Daniel Radcliffe was set to play Harry Potter. The news spread like wildfire on the Internet, television, and in the newspapers. Everyone was buzzing with talk of the new face of Harry Potter. While Dan's parents were worried about their son being thrust into the limelight, Dan was worried about how his friends would take the news. Fortunately they were all very cool about it. "I didn't actually tell any of my friends. I was going to, but they phoned me first because they had seen it on the news . . . they reacted so well and none of them—not one single person—was jealous," he told PBS Online.

Perhaps the reason everyone was so happy for Dan was because he kept his humble, low-key attitude, despite the fact that the news about him was circulating fast.

So humble, Dan couldn't even understand why he had gotten the role in the first place. "I don't know why they chose me," Dan said on the *Today* show in 2001. "But I'm glad they did."

Chris couldn't have been happier. From the moment he saw *David Copperfield*, Chris knew Dan would be perfect for the role, and Dan had turned out to be everything he had hoped. "There's such a sense that he has lived a life, a much more mature life than most kids his age," Chris told the *Detroit News* of Daniel. "There's just such depth in his eyes." That kind of look is usually reserved for kids who have seen a lot of trouble in their lives, which couldn't have been further from Dan's experiences in his nurturing family environment. Chris was shocked by the complexity the young actor displayed, "because he comes from two very loving parents who support him and who keep him real and keep him grounded," he commented to CNN. However, that is the test of an actor's talent and abilities, and it was clear that Daniel passed this test with flying colors. It became apparent very early on that Daniel would amaze them in many more ways in the years to come.

Having worked with children before in movies such as *Goonies* and *Home Alone*, Chris knew that Dan would be able to weather the storm of attention that was headed his way at about one hundred miles per hour, which is an important ability to have when you are in the spotlight. "One thing I learned after dealing with child actors was cast the parents as well," he said on *Today*. "I realized when I met Dan's parents that they were so focused on being great parents, and I knew that Dan would come through this okay."

But what would J. K. Rowling, the ultimate Harry Potter expert, think of Dan? When she received the tape of Dan's audition performance, she called David Heyman. This phone call was a crucial moment. What would happen if J. K. Rowling did not think Daniel was right for the part? Would they have to recast Harry? It all rested in this one phone call. David shared their conversation with the *Detroit News*, describing her voice as wavering with emotion when she told him, "I feel like I've reunited with my long-lost son." Dan could not have received a bigger endorsement.

With J. K.'s approval and the role officially, one hundred percent his, Dan had to spend some serious time with the first three big books. He admitted to the *Detroit News* in 2001, "I never really enjoyed reading." Like most kids in Britain, Dan had read the first two *Harry Potter* books when he was about eight and nine years old. He liked them fine, but truthfully, he has admitted to the *Detroit News*, "I wasn't obsessed." But after he got the part, it was a different story. He dove back into J. K. Rowling's books and read the first three all over again. "*Now* I'm obsessed," he said. He loved them so much the second time around that he credits them with helping him read more in general. "They've really helped me to branch off into other books," he said on *Today*.

The books also helped him with his acting. Dan told Katie Couric on *Today* that figuring out how to play Harry Potter was a breeze, since J. K. had put everything down in writing. "You don't necessarily have to put . . . your own twist to it, because it's such a well-defined character in the books," he confessed. "All the explanation you need to play—it's really in the book. So I don't have to do much work, really."

That's what Dan said, but he had no idea what was

in store for him once he met up with the entire crew and cast, including eleven-year-old Rupert Grint, who was cast to play Ron Weasley, and ten-year-old Emma Watson as Hermione Granger. J. K. gave her blessing to them all, telling the *San Francisco Chronicle*, "I wish Dan, Emma, and Rupert the very best of luck and hope that they have as much fun acting the first year at Hogwarts as I had writing it."

5   FILM WIZARDS

There was no question that Dan was a mature kid, an old soul in a child's body, as David Heyman had wished for. But millions of discerning and skeptical Potter fans of all ages were waiting to be convinced that Dan could live up to the fictional character that they all adored. For many kids, Harry Potter was a hero, a symbol of goodness and a fighter of evil. Fans feared that the Harry they would see on-screen would fall short of their expectations, and shatter the character they loved, but at the same time they hoped Dan would prove their fears wrong and give them the real-life Harry they all wanted to see. That's a lot of pressure for an eleven-year-old kid to handle!

Dan had been so swept up in the excitement of getting the role and rehearsing with his new cast mates and director, that he almost forgot about the outside pressures and social expectations associated with the huge project. But it all kind of hit him right at the moment when he needed to be on the top of his game—the first day of shooting. He got really nervous while the makeup artist was applying the famous Harry Potter scar to his head. Up until that point, he had just been doing read-throughs of the script with Rupert, Emma, and Chris in Chris's office. No big deal. But now he glanced down at the call sheet for the first day of filming and read his name, Rupert's, and Emma's. Then he turned the page and read, EXTRAS, 150.

"At that moment, I got quite scared," he admitted to BBC Online. As he explained to E! Online, "I realized I was about to step in front of the camera with hundreds of people around." Dan had hit the big time: lights, camera, action!

The fact that Dan had J. K. Rowling's stamp of approval almost made the pressure worse. As he told CNN later, in 2001, he hoped that he didn't go in there and "just kind of muck it up completely." He had a right to be nervous. There were the millions of expectant fans, the rumors running rampant on Harry Potter Web sites and in chat rooms, all about who this Daniel person was and whether or not he could hack it as the famous Harry. And there he was, young Dan, his stomach churning as he sat calmly and quietly at the center of a $125 million production. On a production that big, "mucking it up" wasn't really an option.

An army of cast and crew members was enlisted on the set of *Harry Potter and the Philosopher's/Sorcerer's Stone*— the first in the series, which starts with Harry living under the stairs of his aunt and uncle's house. That's until the giant Hagrid comes to invite him to Hogwarts School of Witchcraft and Wizardry, where he not only meets his best friends but also learns about his magical powers and the truth about his parents. There were 1,600 crew members putting together the sets and assisting in the filming. That's not even counting all the people working in the special-effects houses, who created all the monsters and magic that looked so real in the film.

The film was shot in England, where labor laws limit the number of hours child actors can work per day. Usually on a movie, filming will go on for twelve, sometimes fourteen hours a day. It is a truly exhausting project. But Dan, Emma, and Rupert couldn't work those hours. That meant that the filming went on much longer on this set than it does on most others, and that these folks ended up spending a whole lot of time together. In total, the first Harry Potter movie took a whopping 130 days to shoot (some independent films are shot in two weeks!)

Leavesden Studios in Hertfordshire, England, once a World War II aircraft-assembly plant, was transformed into the mammoth sets that made up the film's magical atmosphere. Leavesden has been the setting of a lot of great movies. It was used in the Star Wars film *Attack of the Clones* and the Bond flick *Die Another Day*. According to production designer Stuart Craig (who won three Oscars, including one for his work on *Gandhi*), it took the equivalent of thirty-one years in manpower to make the Hogwarts School set. The plaster was pouring. In fact, more of that stuff was used in *Philosopher's/Sorcerer's Stone* than was used to create the sets in the Roman-era epic *Gladiator*.

Only the top people from the movie business were hired to bring this project to life. Basically, if you didn't have an Academy Award nomination, you could forget about joining the crew. John Seale was the director of photography. In his twenty-five-year career, he had directed the photography on amazing films such as *Dead Poets Society, The Talented Mr. Ripley*, and *The English Patient*, for which he won an Oscar. Otherwise known as the cinematographer, John was responsible for all the artistic and technical decisions related to the photography on a film, from what lens to use on the camera to what type of lighting scheme to use.

Judianna Makovsky was hired as the costume designer for her fifteen years of experience in making costumes for the most beautiful stars in Hollywood, including Gwyneth Paltrow, Nicole Kidman, and Sandra Bullock. For this film she turned her talents from the glamorous to quirky and sometimes downright frightening looks.

Although it was far from his typical outfit of a T-shirt and jeans, Dan looked adorable in the clothing Judianna created for his character. There was definitely an edge to his Hogwarts tie, jacket, and famous striped scarf that took it beyond the typically dowdy school uniform. Even his big round eyeglasses—which could easily have looked superdorky—came off as cool.

From scratch, crew members built the elaborate Great Hall that was big enough to fit 350 little wizards-in-training. When all was said and done and the Great Hall came to life, J. K. was immensely pleased with what she saw. Although she was consulted often on the film, she only visited the set once. "There are, for sure, going to be people out there who are going to say that 'this is not my Great Hall,'" she told the *Philadelphia Inquirer* in 2001. "But I can promise them, it is *my* Great Hall."

The craftsmanship of the Diagon Alley set was so detailed and complex that it easily could have been mistaken for a real street. No detail was spared. In Wiseacres Wizarding Equipment shop, a sign told customers that dragon liver and clabbert pustules were the special of the day. The Ollivanders wand shop, another boutique in Diagon Alley, was stocked with more than sixteen thousand wand boxes and had its very own fancy shopping bags that the set dresser had created. Those wands certainly didn't lose their value after the movie wrapped. Two of the wands used during the filming were sold at an auction, bringing in more than $18,000. Harry Potter fans are detail junkies and wouldn't have settled for less. In fact, because the book has two different titles, two versions were shot of every single scene where the stone is mentioned.

The prop that gave the real-life wizards behind the film's production a major headache was the Whomping Willow (which inspired its own Web site). The violent tree is planted in the middle of the school grounds and, as is revealed later on in the series, hides an opening to a secret passage that goes from Hogwarts to the Shrieking Shack in the wizarding village of Hogsmeade. The tree, which the Weasleys' flying car eventually smashes into, was a complex combo of hydraulics and special effects.

One of the most involved scenes in the film was the amazing Quidditch game where Harry and the rest of his schoolmates ride around on broomsticks, trying to keep from getting their heads knocked off by balls known as Bludgers, while Harry tries to accomplish the goal of catching the winged Golden Snitch. That game, which practically zips by in the movie, lasting about nine minutes in total, took three months to plan and another six whole months to shoot! But Dan loved every high-flying minute. "We went very fast, very high, and I really was sitting on a broom," he told the *Detroit News* in 2001. Other than the fun he had, Dan's lips were sealed about the scene's secret special effects. But he did reveal that his favorite prop from the film was the Nimbus Two Thousand, his speedy flying broomstick. Why that one? "It is the fastest broom you can buy and makes all of Harry's friends and people who aren't so friendly to him very, very jealous," he revealed on *Today*.

The amazingly rendered sets and special effects were combined with real footage from some beautiful—and very old—places around England, including the Bodleian Library, Christ Church College, and Gloucester Cathedral. Filming at real places gave the film an authenticity that couldn't be matched by even the most skilled of production designers.

They also shot at Alnwick Castle in Scotland and in Dan's hometown of London. There, at King's Cross Station, they filmed the scene where Harry walks through a brick pillar to Platform 9 3/4 so he can catch the Hogwarts Express that leaves from the station only once a year.

Even though Dan was filming right in the city where he lived, he still could only keep in touch with friends via e-mail and text messages. Between shooting, getting tutored on set, and returning home to sleep, there was no time for Dan to fool around with friends from school, even if they weren't very far away.

6   NEW FRIENDS ON SET

With a fantastic set and special effects in place, the only thing left to do was to fill *Harry Potter and the Philosopher's/Sorcerer's Stone* with an equally fantastic cast. The film was not only going to be shot in England, it also had to have an all-British cast. Director Chris Columbus insisted on this from the get-go. As he had said from the start, he didn't want to Americanize the distinctly British vibe of the books.

Usually the most experienced people, having proved they can carry a film, get the lead roles. But in *Harry*

Potter, everything was turned on its head. Absolute first-timers were paired with screen legends, and the newbies were the ones who took center stage.

Out of the three young lead actors, Dan had the most film experience. And he had only made one major film at that point! Rupert and Emma were completely fresh faced. Neither had done any professional acting at all. The extent of their acting experience was in school plays. Despite their lack of experience, both Emma and Rupert seemed to blow the casting directors away with their ability to portray the characters of Hermione and Ron. What sealed the deal was the fact that they worked well with Dan on-screen. "They just fit," Chris told the *Philadelphia Inquirer*.

The three Gryffindors fit on-screen because, in real life, Dan told E! Online, "We all really like each other." That's important since they had to spend so much time together during that first movie, and then eventually over the years making its many sequels. One of the threesome's favorite scenes was filmed on the Hogwarts Express: It was just the three of them surrounded by tons of candy. They got to laugh, joke, and stuff themselves with sweets without any adults, as Dan would say, to muck it up. Dan credited his good chemistry with Rupert and Emma to the similarities they each shared with their fictional counterparts. "To a certain extent, we're kind of quite like our characters," he told CBS in 2002. "Our characters bond because of who they are, and I think because we're kind of like them. We all bond the same way." Dan and Rupert became really good friends, as did their characters in the film. Sometimes it was hard to tell whether they were acting or being themselves! On occasion they even called each other Ron and Harry offscreen, instead of their real names.

It's true that the young actors' personalities reflected their on-screen characters. Dan was known to be intense and a little serious, much like Harry, with the weight of the world on his shoulders. However, like Harry, Dan isn't afraid to take risks, and he knows when a good practical joke is in order.

Unlike Dan, who didn't take to the Potter books right away, Emma had already read them through and knew the material backward and forward, much like her character Hermione. In fact, Emma was already a crazy fan when casting agents showed up at her school to offer her and a couple of her classmates the chance to audition in the school gym. She was ecstatic when she landed the part of Hermione, a real know-it-all and the smartest student at Hogwarts. Emma can definitely relate to Hermione's bossy tendencies. "I suppose if you'd ask my brother, he'd say I'm really bossy. I'm like her in the way I try hard at school and I enjoy school, but my whole life isn't obsessed with school," she told the *Washington Post*. "Also, she likes cats. I like cats."

On set it took Emma longer to warm up to people, just like her reluctant character Hermione. The Oxford, England, native could, at times, have seemed cold, but that was just until she got to know everyone. It couldn't have been easy being practically the only girl surrounded by hundreds of boy wizards. "I stay on my toes," Emma told *Teen People* magazine in 2002. "Dan and Rupert make funny faces when I'm shooting. But I keep them in line." She was grateful for her friends and family, who kept her grounded to her familiar past. Maybe that's why she spent a lot of time keeping in touch with her buds by phone or e-mail. "They have treated me as a normal person," she said of her friends. "They know me as Emma.

They don't go around calling me Hermione Granger. My parents have been really good about this."

Rupert was a natural ham with great comic instincts. The good-natured redhead dove right into every aspect of the film with great relish, even the part where he gets soaked by Fluffy's (the huge three-headed dog) drool. "It was kind of disgusting but it was wicked," he told the *Ottawa Citizen.* "But I certainly didn't taste it." He also got treated like an ordinary kid, and not a star, when he returned home to his brother and three sisters. "The little ones don't really understand," he laughed. "They just treat me as Rupert, which is good."

Although the three young actors shared a lot in common, they each definitely had different ideas about the best part of their job, which they shared with the *Calgary Sun* in 2002. Emma couldn't wait for the fancy dresses and makeup she would wear to the premieres, but that still wasn't the best part for her. "Take away all the glamour and attention and premieres," Emma said, "it's the acting, and working with fantastic actors and directors." Rupert, ever the comedian, came up with his own answer: "The best was coughing up slugs. . . ." But

Dan had his own thoughts on the best perk of playing Harry Potter. "The best thing is playing a character who has inspired children and adults all over the world," Dan said. That's the typically mature, thoughtful answer one would expect from Dan. It seems as though the three really are very much like their Gryffindor characters!

Alongside these kids, who were coming up with their own ideas about acting for the first time, were famous actors who had been in the business for decades and decades. One of the most unlikely faces in *Philosopher's/Sorcerer's Stone* was Richard Harris, a famous Irish actor who had appeared in over seventy films and television shows. A member of the Royal Shakespeare Company for thirty years, he had been offered the part of Albus Dumbledore, the head of Hogwarts School of Witchcraft and Wizardry, but originally turned it down. At seventy-one, the elderly actor shrank from the thought of committing to a seven-movie series. "I hate commitment," he told the *Washington Post* in 2001. "Hate being tied down. I hate laws and regulations. I'm a rebel. Hate it!" It wasn't the huge paycheck or the accolades that finally convinced him to change his mind. He agreed only after his twelve-year-old granddaughter, Ella Harris, strong-armed him into it. "She's fanatic about Harry Potter," he remembered. "And when she heard I wasn't going to do it, she called me up and said, 'Papa, if you don't do it I'll never speak to you again.'" That worked, but she still couldn't get him to actually read the books. "Not my kind of reading," he complained. "So I got her to sit down and explain it all to me." All Harry Potter fans are thankful to Ella for convincing Richard to take on the role as the wise and lovable Albus.

Dame Maggie Smith, Dan's old pal from *David Copperfield*, also joined the cast as Professor Minerva McGonagall, head of Gryffindor House and the deputy headmistress at Hogwarts. It must have been nice for Dan to be reunited with a familiar face. Dan was quite fond of Maggie. "She's so nice," Dan remarked on *The Caroline Rhea Show*. "She's got such a cool sense of humor. She's really cool." Unfortunately for Harry, Maggie's fictional character wasn't quite as "cool" as the real-life Maggie.

Alan Rickman, whose first major film was *Die Hard* in 1988, took the part of Professor Snape. Robbie

Coltrane was cast as Rubeus Hagrid, Harry's personal guardian giant and the gamekeeper at Hogwarts. The 6'1" Scottish actor often plays giants—with a little help from a computer-generated image, he morphed into the enormous Mr. Hyde in *Van Helsing*. Even with the help of the computer, Robbie still had to wear padding and lifts, and filming from low angles helped add to his bulk and giant-size height.

Chris found these renowned actors from the United Kingdom a breath of fresh air after working with Hollywood stars. "The ones I've worked with here aren't prima donnas, aren't concerned about the size of their trailers, don't bring their cook and fitness coach along," Chris told *Time Out* in 2002. "They're concerned about the work. When they're not here, they go off and do theater. No ego about it. That's refreshing when you're coming from Hollywood where it's all about the paychecks and the billing."

One might think that the acting legends and little kids wouldn't mix, but on the *Harry Potter* set anything could—and did—happen. The elders even tolerated Dan's pranks. One could say the set was kind of like the

Gryffindor common room, except Dan was the one playing practical jokes, not the Weasley twins! One of Dan's favorite pastimes on the set was to fiddle with people's cell phones so that they were translated into foreign tongues. "Everyone on set has a mobile phone, and I found by pushing a few buttons, they could be programmed into different languages," Dan told the *Christian Science Monitor* in 2001. "I fixed Robbie's to speak in Turkish." Robbie's response was to take off after the fleet-footed boy. He didn't even come close to catching him since Robbie was still wearing his costume: a sixty-five-pound leather jacket and twenty-pound platform shoes. At least Dan hadn't put *another* frog in Robbie's boot!

Occasionally Dan was the butt of some on-set jokes. One day Emma and Rupert got the bright idea to print out loads of little signs with clever sayings such as "pull my hair," "kick me," and "I'm sick." They cut out about ten of the little signs and stuck them all over Dan's back without him realizing what was going on. "He walked around for, I don't know, ten minutes without noticing," Emma remembered on *Today*. Everyone was laughing, and Dan, who didn't have a clue about what was going on, couldn't understand why everyone was kicking him. For a stunt like that, Emma and Rupert would have lost loads of points for Gryffindor!

Between the pranks they did for fun, and the hard work they put in actually filming the major motion picture, the kids also had to fit in some schoolwork. Just because you are about to become a worldwide star doesn't mean you can slack off and not do your homework. The year he made *Harry Potter and the Philosopher's/Sorcerer's Stone*, Dan missed everything but the first two weeks of regular school. So the three young actors were tutored between three and five hours a day on set. "I have the most fantastic tutor," Dan told PBS Online. "One-on-one tutoring really, really works because I got the best exams ever in my life." It's probably pretty hard to cheat, too.

Dan didn't regret missing school because he still got to see his friends (the most important part, right?) on the weekends. He also debriefed his best friend from school, Alex Berman, a Harry Potter "fanatic," on a daily basis. "I believe he's read the fourth book six or eight times, which is pretty impressive," Dan told the *Christian Science Monitor*. "Almost every night after the movie started, we'd talk on the phone, and I'd tell him what scenes we had filmed." He and Alex had a lot to talk about every night since Dan found the process of becoming Harry Potter extremely challenging and rewarding. "What I love about playing Harry is that he's a really real character . . . complicated, but he's very accessible," he later told *The Early Show*. "In some films you get . . . broadly drawn characters that are kind of one-dimensional." That wasn't true with this film, where he felt all the characters had "so many different sides."

Dan had always kept in mind the qualities that he and Harry shared and used those similarities to play Harry well. However, there were some aspects of Harry's character that Dan had to try very hard to relate to. The hardest part of becoming Harry, Dan told CNN, was playing "somebody with no parents, who has never even known his parents, because I have a really close relationship with my parents, and we're really good friends." He needed to use his imagination to relate to the experiences of an orphan. Robbie Coltrane realized how difficult this must be for a kid, calling the task "a terrible responsibility for a [child]," as he explained to BBC Online. Robbie saw firsthand how Dan struggled to get the scenes right, when so much was riding on his performance. "It took him a wee bit longer to get the character," he told the *Philadelphia Inquirer*. "He's a nice kid—a lot like Harry, actually. And he and Rupert formed a brilliant bond, which is perfect, really, because Harry is a bit too intense at times, and Ron takes it out of him."

There was also the difficulty of acting with all the special effects. Dan had to deliver lines to people who weren't even there. "It requires a lot of concentration," Dan told Masterpiece Theatre Online. Sometimes he would get a little help. In the scenes with ghosts, Dan explains, "There was Chris Columbus and another man who are doing the voices for the ghosts and they're doing them so well that you kind of feel that they are there."

One thing he didn't have a problem with was learning his lines. "It's more the movement and the choreography and the facial expressions you use with the line," he described as the challenge to Masterpiece Theatre Online. "The lines, you keep going over them. . . . After a while they really sink in."

No matter what kind of problems arose during filming, the three young actors figured out how to overcome them, whether the solution involved humor, more hard work and practice, or the maturity to know when to turn to someone to ask for help. Richard Harris, for one, was truly impressed. He praised Dan, telling BBC Online, "Dan was so instinctive, and so right."

With praise, however, sometimes comes arrogance, and with stardom, sometimes comes the highfalutin Hollywood attitude. Fortunately, it seems like these kids would much rather remain the sweet, reserved, well-mannered people they were when they first walked on the set. As Chris Columbus told the *Chicago Sun-Times*, "[Dan] has much more confidence as an actor although as a person, he's still a shy kid. He still thanks me after each take. You never get Julia Roberts thanking you after each take."

7   WILD ABOUT HARRY

The premiere of *Harry Potter and the Philosopher's/ Sorcerer's Stone*, on November 3, 2001, marked the date that Dan's life would change forever. A huge tidal wave of attention was headed directly for this quiet and graceful young man. He really had no idea what was in store for him, and though he tried to keep his composure in the face of an uncertain future, he must have had his doubts. Would he be able to keep his cool? Or would he lose it on the red carpet? Nobody knew for sure.

On the cusp of becoming the most famous child actor, probably ever, Dan pondered whether or not he was prepared. "I don't know," he softly confessed to the *Philadelphia Inquirer*. "I don't know. I am just going to take it as it comes."

What other choice did he have? Just a kid, Dan still had the protection of his family throughout the experience of premiering the movie around the world. His father set his career as a literary agent aside and became Dan's full-time chaperone. The young actor also had a tight group from the movie—including producer David Heyman and director Chris Columbus—that was ready to shield him from the sometimes harsh and unflattering glare of fame's light.

Despite the nerves he experienced, he was definitely relieved and happy to finally see the fruit of all that hard work up on the big screen. "You give your all for ten months, and then you finally see it, and it's a great moment when you actually see the movie completed," he told the *Toronto Sun* in 2002.

Now worldwide excitement was brewing. Everyone else wanted to see the movie as well. Dan understood the magic of *Harry Potter*, why the film had the ability to elicit this kind of frenzied anticipation. "Not only myself,

© 2002 Getty Images

Daniel gets together with Emma Watson and Rupert Grint at a photo shoot for *Harry Potter and the Chamber of Secrets.*

Here's the trio at a London press conference in 2000.

© 2000 Getty Images

© 2001 Getty Images

Young Daniel playing Harry in the first Harry Potter movie.

Director Alfonso Cuarón appears with his star at the US premiere of *Harry Potter and the Prisoner of Azkaban* in New York.

© 2001 Getty Images

J. K. Rowling makes an entrance with the terrific trio at the London premiere of *Harry Potter and the Philosopher's/Sorcerer's Stone*.

Two cool wizards at the London premiere of *Harry Potter and the Prisoner of Azkaban*!

© 2004 Dave M. Bennet

© 2000 Getty Images

Daniel, Emma, and Rupert at a photo shoot for their first Harry Potter movie.

Daniel gets a laugh out of Chris Columbus, who directed the first two Harry Potter movies.

© 2000 AFP

but I think everybody can relate to Harry in some way," he told the *Today* show. "It's the idea of magic, when magic kind of comes to life, there's so much opportunity for absolutely anything to happen."

As if the built-in audience of millions of book lovers wasn't enough, the movie studio, Warner Bros., launched one of the biggest publicity campaigns in history. Billboards of Dan were plastered everywhere from London's double-decker buses to the office buildings of downtown Manhattan. Despite the publicity Dan always kept his cool, no matter how famous he got. Even to this day, Dan still has difficulty acknowledging his fame. In fact, the young British actor insists that he is just like any normal teenager—well, almost. "I'm kind of just going through what every other teenager goes through—but with posters," he told the *Chicago Sun-Times* in 2004. "It's not as different as people would expect, I don't think, for me, anyway."

When *Philosopher's Stone* premiered, there were Harry Potter products on every shelf, including lunchboxes, Lego sets, and specially made jelly beans with the name "Bertie Bott's Every Flavor Beans," mimicking the film's

miraculous candy that comes in every flavor from chocolate to ear wax to liver. AOL Time Warner, the company
that owned Warner Bros. at the time, teamed up with a
number of other big companies to help promote *Harry
Potter* the movie and Harry Potter the brand. Coca-Cola
partnered with the film in a $150-million advertising
deal that allowed it to sell soda using images from the
movie. That's more than the film's entire budget! One
industry analyst in *Variety* estimated that *Harry Potter and
the Philosopher's/Sorcerer's Stone* would reap $300 million
in profits during its first year, and that the full series of
movies' profit could hit $2 billion. That made Dan one
important kid.

The business honchos didn't want a single living being
to miss the fact that *Harry Potter* was hitting the movie
theater. At the time of the film's release, AOL Time
Warner executive Richard Parson told the *Philadelphia
Inquirer*, "You're not going to be able to go anywhere
without knowing about it. This could be a bigger franchise than Star Wars." He wasn't kidding.

Everyone hopped on the Harry Potter bandwagon. Leading
up to the premiere, English newspapers had daily Harry

Potter features and tidbits on their front pages. Television news crews crowded around King's Cross train station to film the spot where the Hogwarts Express departs once a year. A survey from that time showed that Harry Potter had jumped ahead of Sherlock Homes, Oliver Twist, Winnie the Pooh, and even James Bond as the most famous character in British literature. All this didn't go unnoticed by the British Tourist Authority, which published maps of the various historic locations captured in the film, hoping to entice people from all over the world to visit England.

Like the publishers who made sure there were millions of copies ready when a new *Harry Potter* hits bookstores, so Warner Bros. made sure the film played in as many theaters as possible when it opened. *Harry Potter and the Philosopher's/Sorcerer's Stone* was set to play in 131 countries, in forty different languages. In the U.S. alone, *Harry Potter and the Sorcerer's Stone* played on a record-breaking 8,200 movie screens across the country on opening day. Dan was in store for a ride bumpier than any game of Quidditch could ever be.

8   THE BIG TIME

More than ten thousand fans gathered to scream and swoon when Dan arrived at the world premiere of *Harry Potter* in London. At the momentous event, Dan watched the film for the third time. Although he loved the final product, he hated seeing himself on the screen, especially that evening. "I hate watching myself. I really really hate it," he told CNN, but at the London premiere it was even worse, or as he said, "quite frightening because there were so many people there."

There were a lot of people who would weigh in on this film, but perhaps there was no one more important than J. K. Rowling. She made her firm pronouncement after seeing the film. "I think Dan nailed it," she said in a written statement later published by the *Toronto Star*, "and I am really pleased." Crowds around the world roared.

But not everyone agreed that the film was a hit. The critical reviews were definitely mixed. In Britain, Dan and his fellow cast members received a lot of praise. Still, not every paper liked it. London's *Guardian* newspaper lamented, "*Harry Potter* has joined the pantheon of films judged to be Not as Good as the Book." Back in America, *The Sorcerer's Stone* got the big thumbs-down from reviewers. They saw it as just another soulless Hollywood blockbuster. "The American press was pretty vicious," director Chris Columbus told the *Chicago Sun-Times*. "Some critics thought this was a corporate movie set out to make zillions, but that's not true. To us it's art." Well, there's no accounting for taste. At least Chris's harshest critics—his daughter and her friends—thought his film was really cool.

Film reviewers weren't the only ones who criticized *The Philosopher's/Sorcerer's Stone*. Some adults felt that all the magic and weird mystical stuff in the film seduced young audiences to become fixated on the occult. The British Association of Teachers and Lectures—a 150,000-member organization—put out a warning that the film could cause children to become obsessed with the dark arts. This controversy had started with the Harry Potter books, which hit the American Library Association's list of the Most Frequently Challenged Books of 1990–2000 for this very same reason.

Dan dismissed those accusations as being completely absurd. "I can't see how it's Satanism or anything," he told the *Toronto Sun*. "The only thing that saves Harry from being killed is the love his mother had for him. How can that be judged as evil?" He explained that the film's central theme was "redeeming love," not "sorcery."

Any controversy over witchcraft didn't seem to keep people from going out to see *Harry Potter and the Philosopher's/Sorcerer's Stone*, that's for sure. It was an undeniable commercial triumph. Blowing the expert from *Variety*'s predictions out of the water, the film took in close to $1 billion. Before the film even opened in North America, it had sold several hundred thousand advance tickets, according to reports. There were Harry Potter fanatics who went out and saw the first film twenty-three times! Dan also received a bunch of prestigious awards, including the Variety Club of Great Britain's Best Newcomer Award and Italy's David di Donatello Award.

Along with his awards and praise also came some harsh critiques. Check out the response to Dan's hair, when he was only twelve years old! Because J. K. Rowling had depicted the main character's hair as "all over the place," stylists gave Dan a bunch of haircuts so it would resemble that description. But no matter how many haircuts he got, his brown locks always fell neatly into place. Sad to say, Dan had a bowl cut. Most normal kids would only get ribbed by their mates for a bad haircut, but Dan had to deal with worldwide press on his nerdy style. "Daniel has a pudding bowl hairdo," wrote London's *Sunday Express* columnist

Anna Pukas. "In fact, he looks like a girl." Ouch! The lame hairstyle wasn't even his choice.

Overnight Dan went from ordinary kid to worldwide star, just as everyone had predicted. Throughout his career he has tried to diminish his celebrity. "I don't really consider myself famous," he told Scholastic's Web site. "People like Anthony Hopkins and Robert De Niro are famous because they're very experienced and amazing actors." But there was no denying his star stature, which he knew he had to take somewhat seriously. "How many boys my age get to be a part of all these films and have their faces on buses and billboards?" he asked. Not many.

He was pretty nervous about having to walk down red carpets and travel to fancy hotel rooms for interviews with journalists who came from nearly every paper on the surface of the globe. His life became a whirlwind of television appearances on major network shows and star-studded movie premieres. Big bodyguards and groups of publicists were constantly by his side. He had come a long way from the little boy who sat between his parents at the theater that fateful night.

Despite the exterior transformation, Dan didn't feel that inside he and his young costars were any different from when they had started out. "We probably have changed as actors, but I'm not conscious of myself changing," he related to the *Chicago Sun-Times*. He was proud of this fact and gave a lot of the credit to his parents, who he said didn't lecture, but were there to support him every step of his remarkable adventure. "My mum and dad have just told me to enjoy it," he told BBC Online. "There are a lot worse things [that could] happen than just being recognized."

Emma agreed with her cute leading man, telling blackfilm.com, "I do everything that I used to do. I play sports. I go to normal teenage parties. All of my money is locked away in a bank until I'm twenty-five and I'm not going to see it until then. And I suppose I just have good friends and family who keep my feet on the ground." And they keep Emma from spending all her money on clothes and makeup! Out of the three, she felt the most uncomfortable with her massive celebrity. "I don't like the idea of everyone knowing my face or walking down the street and having people say,

'Oh my god, you're Hermione!'" she told the *Ottawa Citizen*. I guess she should have thought of that before starring in the biggest film sensation of the decade!

Rupert, for one, loved all the attention he was getting. "Getting recognized is pretty cool," he said. "I got recognized when I was in Switzerland, up a mountain. That was amazing." There was nowhere these stars could hide, not even on mountaintops!

In addition to getting recognized, these kids got loads of fan mail. Letters poured in for Dan from all over the world. Everywhere the cast was overwhelmed by the response they received. When any of them had a birthday, those same fans sent lots of presents. "The effort put in is just so amazing," Dan said to the *Toronto Sun* about the thoughtfulness of these strangers sending gifts. However, Dan's mother, Marcia, isn't as impressed by the effort. Every day around 4:00 p.m., she says, the doorbell of their home rings and then she hears, "Does Daniel live here?" She replies yes, but, as she said, "In a tone that will make them never, ever, come back." The fans protest, saying they are carrying presents. But Marcia doesn't soften and just tells them to leave the gifts in the mailbox. "The fans know our address, the names of the dogs, the color of our walls," Marcia told the U.K.'s *Sunday Times*. "I find the level of obsession bizarre."

Because Dan was no longer completely ordinary (come on, riding around in limos with thousands of girls waiting for you wherever you go isn't exactly a typical teen's life), he decided to reinterpret what it means to be a normal kid. "Some people think that because of the weight . . . that I won't have a normal childhood," he told CBS. "For me, a normal childhood isn't necessarily going to school every day. A normal childhood is just like having loads of fun." A lot of kids would probably love to be "normal" according to Dan's definition.

With a tour of premieres all over the world, Dan got to travel to places that few people ever do. Once he even took a helicopter to a premiere! "I feel very privileged to have visited so many countries and seen some of the most amazing sights in the world," he said on the Warner Bros. official Harry Potter Web site. There was one small downside to all this success: autographs.

"I don't like writing my name," Dan admitted to the *Detroit News*. "It's just too long. I have to find a way to write it shorter."

A lot of girls would settle for a kiss instead of an autograph from Dan, if that would be shorter. In the period of time between the filming of *Harry Potter and the Philosopher's/Sorcerer's Stone* and its release, Dan grew two inches and his voice lowered an octave. He was changing from the sweet young kid who had landed the Harry Potter audition and growing into a bona fide hottie whom the girls were gaga over, and these adoring girls would do just about anything to get a glimpse of Dan. But when asked what he thought about being a sex symbol, Dan told the *Toronto Sun*, "Personally, I can't actually see it, but if other people can, then great!" His humble attitude only makes him even cuter.

At one public event, an overeager female fan arrived wearing nothing but a towel. She held up at a sign that read, "Nothing comes between me and Harry Potter." Dan, who is practically the shyest guy on earth, didn't know what to make of this kind of attention. Luckily, she was talking about the Harry Potter towel she was wearing and not the real-life actor before her, which Dan told the *Chicago Sun-Times*, "made me feel better."

Still, it was quite a greeting for a teenage boy, and only the beginning of what will come his way as Daniel's fame continues to grow.

9 MOVING ON

Dan didn't have any time to get a big star attitude from all this attention since filming on the next movie in the series, *Harry Potter and the Chamber of Secrets*, began almost as soon as the production on the first one wrapped. That's because as soon as the first film was screened, Harry Potter devotees were begging for the second one. Director Chris Columbus's kids voiced this impatient attitude. "The minute my kids saw the first film, the pressure was already on me," he told the *Chicago Sun-Times*. "I heard, 'Okay, Dad, now how long do we have to wait for the second one?'"

The second film corresponds to Harry's second year at Hogwarts, where his friendship with Ron Weasley and Hermione Granger picks up at the point it left off. So do the adventures and misadventures that naturally come when a wizard is learning how to master his magic wand. If the first story set up Harry's new life after he escaped Muggleland, then the second one shows that Hogwarts and the magic life isn't always as simple as a game of Quidditch. "The second movie focuses on the fact that his new home and family is in danger and Harry has to save it," producer David Heyman explained to the *Chicago Sun-Times*. "Harry is much more in control this time." Danger lurks everywhere right from the beginning, when Dobby the house-elf warns him not to return to Hogwarts, where eventually he will see many of his fellow students mysteriously petrified.

Chamber of Secrets provided a special challenge for Dan and the team since it is known as one of the least popular books in the series. The first and third books were mega hits, but *Chamber of Secrets* had something the others didn't—a superscary scene with thousands of spiders and a gigantic snake. As Chris told the *Chicago Sun-Times*, he jumped on that scene and he developed it into not one, but a few "full-blown, mega-action scenes for Harry and his friends." The action was so intense that even Rupert told the *Toronto Sun*, "I was scared." But Rupert's main foe was slime. "I had to try out all this different flavored slime—orange, lemon, peppermint and chocolate," the always good-natured redhead said. "They made it taste really nice. I quite liked it." That was pretty thoughtful of the production staff to provide Rupert with tasty goop.

Despite Rupert's run-ins with giant spiders and slug slime, Dan really got the best action in this flick. The greatest challenge for Dan, in terms of special effects, was when he had to act opposite an orange ball that stood in for the computerized house-elf Dobby. It's hard to tell what kind of expression an orange ball has. But despite the challenge, Dan enjoyed acting those scenes very much. "I loved doing the Dobby scenes," Dan told the Warner Bros. official Harry Potter Web site. "I talked to an orange ball at the end of a stick. It was very detailed work because as he bounced around

I had to ensure that my eye line was in exactly the right position. It was demanding."

Another difficult scene comes when Harry has to fight a hideous wizard-bred monster, the basilisk, an eighty-foot serpent who lives in the Chamber of Secrets. In real life the crew built twenty-five feet of the monster. "It was hard to fight," Dan told the *Toronto Sun*. But this wasn't because the basilisk fought back. "I kept knocking its teeth out. They spent endless hours repairing it."

If the filming of *Philosopher's/Sorcerer's Stone* seemed like an enormous undertaking, the *Chamber of Secrets* 150-day shoot was even harder. "It's tough on the kids," David told the *Chicago Sun-Times*. "They work a nine-hour day including three hours for education and an hour for lunch. It's a very long process because these kids live in this world for months on end."

By the time the second film was in production, the kids had already begun to grow and change, both physically and emotionally. Going through puberty as an actor poses many challenges. Dan's voice broke during the filming of *Chamber*. Luckily, it wasn't so easily detectable in the movie because his voice jumped from one octave to another, instead of yo-yoing up and down like most pubescent boys' voices do. Dan explained that it made his character even more realistic. He laughed it off, telling *People* in 2002, "Harry's also at an age where his voice might start to break, so I don't think it's a big problem."

No matter what challenge Dan was trying to overcome, fellow actor Robbie Coltrane always kept spirits up on the set with his continuous good humor. When people were dying of boredom after days and days of filming, Robbie had them in stitches, dancing the cancan and the Macarena on a table in the Great Hall. "It was the highlight of the whole filming," Emma told Scholastic.com. But Dan seemed to appreciate it more than anybody else. "[Robbie] seems to have a new joke each time, which I tend to steal and go and tell to everybody else," Dan told *Time Out*.

The first cast had been filled with enough acting greats for ten films, but in the second movie, they added even more. Kenneth Branagh played Gilderoy Lockhart, the egotistical professor of Defense Against the Dark Arts. To fully convey Gilderoy Lockhart's vanity, Kenneth had fifteen costume changes and an office filled with paintings and photos of himself. Initially Hugh Grant, the king of self-centered characters, was considered for the role, but Chris told *Time Out*, "I was concerned that if you were in the world of Hogwarts and Hugh Grant came on-screen, it would feel like a cameo appearance. Ken is playing it very realistically." Realistically for a professor of Defense Against the Dark Arts, that is.

Kenneth also proved handy when it came to preparing Dan for his dueling scene. The young actor picked up his fencing technique from watching Kenneth and Alan Rickman battling it out with swords. "Apparently, there's a certain salute before you start the duel," Dan told Scholastic.com about one of the many cool skills he's acquired since becoming a movie star.

Chamber of Secrets also introduced a new evil character, Draco Malfoy's father, Lucius, who was played by Jason Isaacs. He took his inspiration for Lucius from a real-life conceited art critic. As to his acting method, Jason's motto on this project was the more, the better.

"The fetters are off in magic films," he told *Time Out*. "We try to out-ham each other."

Richard Harris reprised his role as Albus Dumbledore, but unfortunately *Chamber of Secrets* would be his last film; he died of Hodgkin's disease on October 25, 2002. Dan was honored to be in the last scene Richard ever shot. "It was awful," Dan told blackfilm.com of the actor's death. "I don't think Richard is the kind of guy who would've wanted us to mourn over him. He would've wanted us to be happy and just remember him for all the times he made us smile and just laugh." Still, it was hard to go on without him. "He was a perfect Dumbledore," Emma told blackfilm.com. Michael Gambon, who played the role in the next film, put his own, more mischievous stamp on the character. It must have been hard for Dan to cope with the death of someone he had worked so closely with, but he persevered and continued to use whatever he had learned from Richard's great example.

Everyone worked hard on *Chamber of Secrets*—which hit theaters in the fall of 2002—to make it something they would all be proud of. Like its predecessor,

Chamber also grossed nearly $1 billion! "The second film is even better," Dan told CBS, comparing it to the first. "It's a lot darker and a lot edgier." Dan was also just beginning to show his own edgier side to the world.

10   DAN GOES DARK

If Dan liked *Chamber of Secrets* because of its darker tone, he was ecstatic about the next film on his plate because it got a whole lot darker. *Harry Potter and the Prisoner of Azkaban*, the third film in the series, which began production on February 21, 2003, has all the usual evil creatures and strange happenings, but this movie goes to even spookier depths as Harry faces the violent death of his parents in the past and a terrifying killer who is after him in the present. To get into this role, where he confronts his demons, Dan listened to the harsh music of the Sex Pistols, a seminal band whose lead singer, Sid Vicious, died of a drug overdose. As if this weren't enough inspiration for an existential crisis, Dan also watched the films of French New Wave director François Truffaut and Italian director Vittorio De Sica, who made *The Bicycle Thief*, in order to understand his character's hopelessness.

To give the film a fresh look that would correspond to the adolescent angst Dan was preparing for, a new director was invited into the Harry Potter family, and the addition was extremely surprising. Mexican filmmaker Alfonso Cuarón—who made a name for himself with an Oscar nomination for his small, subversive film *Y Tu Mamá También* about two teenage boys who go on a very enlightening road trip—was now put in charge of a mainstream billion-dollar empire. He told *Newsweek* that his version of *Harry Potter* was going to have "lots of nudity. And lots of sex."

Of course, he was only joking. But the new change in director did cause some anxiety among the young actors. Not only was Alfonso best known for making racy films, he also didn't know much about Harry Potter before he got the job. "I hadn't read the books. I hadn't seen the movies," Alfonso admitted to IGN FilmForce. "I knew Harry Potter obviously, but I don't know, for some reason I just thought that it was a big, big kid's franchise. You know? I was not into it." But he changed his tune as soon as he read the script. Alfonso realized just how human these little wizards are. "You can see it as a metaphor about racism and classicism and power," he said. "And also about friendship and loneliness."

Dan, Rupert, and Emma were intimidated by the new director, who blasted mariachi music on the set in England's Hertfordshire countryside to mark hitting the midway point of the shoot. But the original director, Chris Columbus, would never be too far away. He still served as the film's producer. Chris was glad that Alfonso took over. After the first two films, he really needed a break. It was difficult for him to leave, but one day, while directing Dan in a sword fight, Chris realized that if he continued working at that pace, he would definitely die of a heart attack. He also wanted to devote more time to his family. "My own kids are thirteen, ten, eight, and five. Ironically, the same people who got me into these films, which are my own kids, want me out," Chris told the *Chicago Sun-Times*. "They would like to see their father at the dinner table."

Alfonso was lucky to have Chris's example to learn from. One thing that he learned from Chris was to make sure he scheduled enough time to get the special effects just right in *Azkaban*. Chris confessed to *Newsweek* that the effects in *Philosopher's/Sorcerer's Stone* "weren't up to snuff." Alfonso didn't have to hear that twice. His team worked on just the dementors effects alone for six months.

Of the three young stars, Dan was the most disappointed about Chris's departure. It wasn't that he didn't like Alfonso; Dan had just become attached to Chris due to working with him so closely. Still, Dan tried to look on the bright side. "Everything we learned with Chris, we were now able to put into practice with a different director," he told the *Pittsburgh Post-Gazette*. "And it is harder and more challenging, which is good because if we're getting older and we're not being challenged, there's really no point in doing it."

Producer David Heyman explained that Alfonso had the perfect qualifications for making the film that shows

Harry Potter becoming a teenager. "Alfonso has a keen understanding of the nuances of teenage life," he told *Newsweek*. "*Y Tu Mamá* is about the last moments of adolescence, and *Azkaban* is about the first."

There was one perk for Dan and Emma now that Alfonso was their director. Both actors had just started to learn Spanish in school, so they were able to practice with the Mexican director what they had learned during their lessons. "He did teach quite a lot," Dan told IGN FilmForce.

In order to get to know his young actors better, Alfonso gave them homework. Seriously! He made them each write an essay about their own character. Always up for a challenge, they dove into the assignment, writing not only *about* their characters but also as if their characters had completed the essays themselves. Emma, taking on the personality of Miss Perfect Hermione, wrote a detailed eleven-page report that Alfonso read out loud to the other two pupils. Rupert, well, he never handed his in. Hey, that's exactly what Ron would do, right? And Dan wrote a terse one-page summary à la Harry. Well, Cuarón's exercise worked. "That kind of revealed to us how much like our characters we are, and it terrified us," Dan said on BBC's Radio 1.

Alfonso ran the movie in a completely different way. "Alfonso is much more gritty than Chris ever was," Emma noted to *Newsweek*. "He's really into the idea that [shooting] should be fluid and natural. People can be eating an apple during a take." Alfonso's directions brought out powerful reactions and emotions in Dan, Rupert, and Emma, most of which they didn't even know they had in them. Dan compared Chris's style to that of Alfonso on the Warner Bros. official Harry Potter Web site. "Chris is without a doubt, the most energetic director I have ever met. He was amazing in keeping us motivated and in encouraging us every step of the way," Dan remarked. "Alfonso on the other hand directs in a more intense way. The scenes in the film are some of the most passionate and emotional I have worked on and Alfonso's style has been very helpful." Of course, because the three actors were all older, they had naturally developed a greater acting range, and they could do longer takes and more complicated shots. This gave Alfonso more material with which to work.

Though he was sad about the loss of his original director, Dan was overjoyed about the new additions to the cast. Gary Oldman, one of Dan's ultimate heroes, came on as the wizard Sirius Black, an escaped prison inmate who appears to have an ax to grind with Harry Potter. "He's just the best actor of his generation," Dan said on *Today*. "It was really weird for me, meeting him, because as long as I've been acting, I've always been a huge fan of all his movies. And so it was really surreal . . . meeting him." Before filming started, Emma asked Dan who Gary Oldman was. Dan's response? "Dan almost bit my head off," Emma remarked at a press conference in NYC.

As if Dan didn't already idolize Gary enough, the older actor scored major points when they first met on set. Gary, who knew about Dan's passion for music, presented him with a bass guitar as a gift. Gary is a great bass player himself. That clinched it. Dan's fondness turned into full-on worship as Gary not only gave him the guitar, but a few bass lessons as well.

One of Emma's acting icons, Emma Thompson, also joined the cast, signing on to play Sybil Trelawney, professor of Divination. Thompson, who had been married to another *Harry Potter* cast member, Kenneth Branagh, for about five years, is one of only ten actors in the world to have been nominated for both supporting and lead actress Academy Awards in the same year. "I love her," Watson gushed to the *Pittsburgh Post-Gazette*. "She's such a great actress, and she did a really good job with Professor Trelawney." Dan is also a fan of Thompson's, as he told *Parade*. "Emma is wonderful . . . and very, very funny."

What marks *Azkaban* as being so different from the first two Harry Potter films is its emotional content. Dan had to show such a range of emotion, all the moods that teenagers go through—loneliness, self-doubt, and confusion—only on top of the regular teenage angst, Harry has to fight an apocalyptic battle against evil. "I just kind of took what I was feeling and basically just exaggerated [it]," Dan told IGN FilmForce. During the dementor scene by the lake, where Sirius Black is dying and Harry has to save him, Dan got so into his role that he almost fainted! "I do this kind of stupid thing where I forget to breathe properly. . . ." Dan explained on IGN FilmForce.

In *Azkaban*, however, Hermione finally got some action

scenes, namely the scene in which she gives Draco Malfoy a serious pummeling. And Emma relished the chance to show the fierceness of her fists. As *Azkaban* was her favorite book, she wanted her performance to be top-notch. For her, this film was all about Girl Power. "I love every single second of it," Emma exclaimed on IGN FilmForce. "I would have done [the punching scene] for a whole week, but, you know, we got it in a couple of takes." Who knew sweet little Hermione was so violent? When the scene was over, Emma shouted at the director, "Well, I want to do it again! I want to do it again!" Emma wasn't the only one who loved that scene. Dan told IGN Filmforce, "At the premiere everybody cheered when she did it." Dan didn't have any problem seeing his costar take center stage when it came to an action scene. He had plenty of his own, battling lurking monsters, and he was ready to share the wealth.

The third movie was a turning point in the life and future of the Harry Potter series, as well as in the three young actors' careers. While the first two films got mixed reviews, and the "good" ones were really mediocre at best, the third Harry Potter flick blew its audiences, and the critics, away, making the Harry Potter story into a true, cinematic experience. While many reviews called the first two films mere illustrations of the books, critics felt the third movie was strong enough to stand on its own, without the book by its side. James Sanford of the *Kalamazoo Gazette* called *Azkaban* "the most atmospheric, heartfelt, and elegantly eerie installment so far," and went on to write, "'mischief managed' marvelously." Owen Gleiberman of *Entertainment Weekly* wrote that it was "the first movie in the series with fear and wonder in its bones, and genuine fun, too," and Roger Ebert of the *Chicago Sun-Times* remarked, "the world of Harry Potter remains delightful, amusing, and sophisticated." The Harry Potter series, like its three main stars, was coming into its own, and gaining true recognition across the globe among movie critics and film buffs, not just Harry Potter fans. Now that's saying a lot!

11 KEEPING PACE WITH POTTER

Production on the fourth film, *Harry Potter and the Goblet of Fire*, began in the summer of 2004 with yet another director, this time a British one, Mike Newell, who directed *Mona Lisa Smile*. The series should have been called *Harry Potter and the Revolving Directors*, but Alfonso Cuarón didn't have any hard feelings. He told *Entertainment Weekly* that he never planned on doing more than one Harry Potter film. "Frankly," Cuarón told the magazine, "I'm extremely lazy."

Prisoner of Azkaban was a critical and commercial success, but Dan wasn't worried about whether *Goblet of Fire* would measure up. He had no doubt it would. "I really do think they're just kind of . . . getting better and better with each film," he told CBS. "The fourth is going to be even better than the third, just because the story progresses even more and you get more into the characters." Not only do the characters get more involved, but so does the adventure. In *Goblet of Fire*, there are dragons, a fierce tournament against other wizardry schools, and a hedge maze that is a lot more threatening than your average shrubbery. *A lot.* "It's fantastic," Dan said to *Entertainment Weekly*. "I can't wait to get the video game for this one."

Harry Potter and the Goblet of Fire explores the characters' adolescence even further. Ironically, the actors and their characters seem to be going through the same experiences at the same time. As Dan told the *Philippine Daily Inquirer*, "[Harry is] coming to terms with a lot of demons and things. He's forced to face them. He's a lot more vulnerable in this film. Sirius can't do anything because he can't come out of hiding to help Harry. Dumbledore doesn't know what's going on. But the main difference is that Harry is growing up and discovering girls." Sounds a lot like what's been happening to Daniel, too! And it seems like Harry Potter fans are going to see quite a bit of these stars growing up, at least on-screen, that is. According to Mike Newell, that is the aspect of the story that he chose to focus on. Newell explained in the *Philippine Inquirer*, "I watched both of Chris's films and I knew what I was going to do. I watched forty or fifty minutes of Alfonso's film and realized with horror that Alfonso had already done it. . . . So what I did was stop thinking who was first and who was last and that kind of competitive, going up the steps thing, and simply thought to myself, what do you really adore about this story? And you make a film that way. I adored seeing these kids growing up."

Some may wonder how Dan feels about playing Harry after all this time, if his feelings have changed at all since the day he discovered he'd gotten the role and started to cry. Well, it seems that Dan is as happy as ever to still be playing the lovable wizard, and hopes to continue doing so as long as he can. As he told the *Philippine Inquirer*, "I love acting because it's the only thing that I've been really good at. I have more confidence when I'm acting than when I'm doing anything that I would be doing at school, like [maybe] sports or writing." In fact, Dan is enjoying playing Harry so much that according to *USA Today*, he's officially announced that he will return to play Harry in the fifth movie, *Harry Potter and the Order of the Phoenix*.

As for the stunts he has to perform in the fourth flick, Dan couldn't be having more fun! As the plot of the fourth movie involves Harry competing in a tri-wizard competition, Dan has had to perform many strange stunts, one of which took place underwater. According to Mike Newell, it was so hard for Dan to keep his eyes open underwater that they couldn't shoot more than fifteen seconds of film at any given time. Did that stop Dan from having a blast? As Dan told *USA Today*, "It did sting a bit in the eyes, but other than that and the ear infections, it was fantastic."

In another stunt Daniel has to battle a dragon, but he has to slide down a roof fifty feet high to do it! "It was pretty much a vertical drop of about fifty feet," Dan told *USA Today*. "I was on a wire going so fast that my mind didn't have time to catch up with my body and go 'Wow, I'm falling.'" However terrifying it may have been, that didn't stop Dan from enjoying it, as he continued to say, "It was fun after the first take. But at the beginning, I was absolutely terrified." One of the more emotionally challenging scenes of the fourth movie comes when Harry has to come to terms with the death of a fellow contestant, and tell the boy's father that his son has perished. "I had to tap into emotions that I personally never felt," Daniel confessed to USA Today, "that most people never have felt. Because they were challenging, it does make [those scenes] fun."

Keeping up with the making of these movies was grueling, even for the most experienced directors, crew, and actors. A big reason for the rapid timetable of the movie series—other than the fact that the movies aren't arriving in the theaters fast enough for the Harry Potter fans—is that Dan, Emma, and Rupert are getting older at a faster rate than their fictional counterparts. Each film represents a year at Hogwarts, but even with their superfast filmmaking, it took a couple of years for each movie to be made and released. With every film, Dan and the others get a little bit older than they are supposed to be in the books.

The three stars have filmed the fourth movie, and so far Daniel has agreed to stay on for the fifth, but after that, it's anyone's guess. Dan considered what it would be like to play an eighteen-year-old Harry. "I'm just going to take it one book at a time," he told BBC Online. "Harry advances so much in each [school] year, he comes more out of his shell."

Of course, there were downsides to sticking faithfully with Harry. While Rupert was able to find free time to do other movies while shooting the series, there was just no way that Dan could do the same. "As I film practically every day on the movie, it is pretty impossible to fit in other films between times," said Dan, who does try to take advantage of other creative outlets when he can. In 2002 he appeared as the surprise guest in a London play called *The Play What I Wrote*, which was directed by Kenneth Branagh. "It was great fun," Dan remarked on the Warner Bros. official Harry Potter Web site. "And the first time I had been onstage!"

Producer David Heyman admitted that real time will

eventually catch up to them. "There'll come a point where they move on; it's inevitable at some point that they—one, two, or all three—will make the decision to move on," he told the *Pittsburgh Post-Gazette.* "We're just going to keep going as quickly as we can. . . . The time is going to come, and it is going to be difficult, there's no question. James Bond survived, but it's going to be challenging." It's really hard to picture anyone else other than Dan playing Harry Potter.

There was no question that our beloved little kid stars were getting older. The signs were everywhere. While on the set of the third film, during his break from the scene where Harry challenges the ominous Sirius Black, Dan did a drum solo with his magic wand instead of playing childish pranks. Emma placed a sign on her dressing-room door that read, BEWARE, BABE INSIDE.

Alfonso Cuarón, director of *Harry Potter and the Prisoner of Azkaban*, got the first taste of hormones flying on the *Harry Potter* set. "You don't need to encourage it. You allow it to be," he told *Newsweek.* "And believe me, they have a lot of it."

With the stars' newly charged hormones and newfound maturity, of course, comes an interest in dating. So it was only natural that people would start to wonder if Dan and Emma had a crush on each other. Emma had transformed from a little, vivacious pixie into a totally foxy lady. Her hair was always perfectly tousled, and her rosy cheeks and megawatt smile were never marred by a zit. Dan had traded in his girly haircut for his own scruffy look, which even appeared dashing with the tailored suits he favored for public appearances. They looked awesome together, arm in arm, on the red carpet. But Emma downplayed their chemistry. When they had to hug for a scene in *Chamber of Secrets*, Emma told the *Toronto Sun* that it was anything but romantic "to hug someone in front of about three hundred kids and you know, everybody in the whole entire world." Of course Dan was a gentleman about the whole thing, which made it okay. "He could have said, 'Eww! Get off me!' He was very nice." Dan would never have done that to Emma. "I didn't mind at all," he told the *Toronto Sun* about hugging Emma, of course blushing. "Why would I mind?"

Dan and Emma had to deal with people butting into

their personal lives all the time, and as the stars grow older and more famous, the public interest in their personal lives will only increase. Dan blushes anytime someone asks him about his love life. He has never been tied to anyone special (it's pretty hard to find time for a date when you are racing to make seven movies), but he is interested in girls. And girls are super interested in him. Dan gets shy, and red-faced, when asked about girls he likes, but it's even worse when he's asked about all the girls who like him. At an event to promote *Prisoner of Azkaban* at New York's Radio City Music Hall, Alfonso introduced everyone in the cast and invited them onto the stage. But it was when Dan walked from stage left to center stage that the crowd of girls went wild, yelling and snapping pictures. "I'm not complaining," Dan admitted on IGN FilmForce.

12   JUST A REGULAR KID

Some teenagers get enormous heads just because they make the cheerleading squad. Can you imagine how those kids would behave if they got love notes from around the world, made millions of dollars, and wore designer clothing to Hollywood's hottest parties? Well, not these teenagers. They love to take off their fancy duds, put on some jeans, and hang out with their normal school friends. They love to just be themselves. Makeup and attention all seems very cool, but like anything else, too much of a good thing gets old quickly.

You might be surprised to find out that Dan likes to do most of the same things that any ordinary kid likes to do. "As far as I am concerned, I am a normal person," he told the Warner Bros. official Harry Potter Web site. "I go out with my friends. I go to the cinema—all the normal things that teenagers do. There is an assumption that I cannot leave my house without being hounded. That is not the case. I am able to do many more things than people think I can."

When he returns home from the set, it's almost like he was never away, since Dan is really into keeping up with all his buddies through e-mail and text messaging. "All my friends treat me exactly the same as they always have, and we always do exactly the same stuff," he told CBS. In fact, if you were to see Dan at home with his friends, you might very well catch him playing Harry Potter games on PlayStation. "I've been killed by Voldemort a lot," he admitted to *Time Out*.

He loves pizza and often will get together with friends for pizza parties where literally all they do all day is eat and "be lazy," he said. It's pretty understandable that a guy who is busy most of the time going to school and having an A-list film career in arduous action-adventure flicks might want to just veg out once in a while.

When Dan is filming Harry Potter, he has a pretty strict schedule. His day starts at 7:30 a.m. when a studio car comes to pick him up at his home. His dad, Alan, goes with him, while his mom, Marcia, stays home to work, exercise, and make Dan's bed! Alan, who gave up his position as a literary agent to chaperone his son, doesn't mind his new job. "He sees it as a privilege to have given up a stressful job to spend so much time with his son," Marcia told the U.K.'s *Sunday Times Magazine* in 2003. With filming and tutoring on set, he and his dad don't get home until about 7:30 p.m. It's a long day, but no one is complaining. "We all enjoy what Dan's doing to the max," Marcia went on to say. "To be honest, Warner Bros. makes our lives easy. They provide a brilliant tutor, they even delayed filming the latest film so he could start at his new school and have one term being normal."

That's what Marcia thinks, but Dan still has to work all day. So when he gets home from the set, it's straight to the sitting room where he eats his dinner in front of the TV (watching *The Simpsons,* of course, what else?).

"It's his only chance to unwind," his mother explained. Despite the long days, Marcia admitted that, "After a break between films, he can't wait to get back."

It's also surprising that although his name and face are known all over the world, Dan still gets starstruck. Big name celebrities flock to the premieres of his movies, to see *him* on the screen, but Dan still acts like he just caught an accidental glimpse of them at the mall. He said that the best thing about being famous was meeting Ben Stiller, the hilarious comic and star of many funny movies, at the London opening of *Chamber of Secrets*. A close second was meeting the famous couple Tim Robbins and Susan Sarandon at the New York premiere. There are still a lot of people he hopes to meet. They include actor Philip Seymour Hoffman, who has starred in *Boogie Nights*, *Magnolia*, and many other movies. Dan is dying to meet cartoonist Matt Groening. "I'm absolutely obsessed with *The Simpsons*," he told the *Washington Post*.

Sure Dan's life seems like a dream, but he does have a lot of stresses. Becoming a teenager has only added to them. Still, no one has ever seen him throw a tantrum on the set or slam his trailer door shut. He never fights with any of his costars or crew members. Out of all the millions of fans that he's met, there has never been a report of him snapping at any of them. That's because he has a surefire way of dealing with all those new hormones raging within him, as Dan told blackfilm.com. "Hormones are interesting things . . . I listen to a lot of rock music, which I think does help to let off a lot of steam, definitely." When he was promoting *Chamber of Secrets* at the Essex House hotel in New York, he told reporters, "To be honest with you, I'd rather be at home in my room right now listening to punk rock music."

Not surprising are Dan's sophisticated tastes. He likes music from bands that broke up way before he was even born. But Dan has been hanging around adults on film sets for a long time now, and has picked up a thing or two. He also is the only child of two very sophisticated parents, who took him to the theater regularly and exposed him to a lot. Dan wasn't going to settle for any Britney Spears or the latest boy band. Instead Dan is into edgier stuff. In fact, with his main musical passion, punk, he doesn't even like current bands. He spends all his time listening to the Sex Pistols, the New York Dolls, and the Stranglers, all punk bands from when the term "punk" was just invented. "I like the attitude. Yeah!" he told *Time Out*. One of the only current bands he gave a few props to was the Hives.

Dan's other extracurricular love is movies—not being in them, although he thinks that's pretty cool as well, but watching them. When he was a little kid, one of his favorite films was *Dead Poets Society,* about young boys coming of age under the tutelage of a character played by Robin Williams. "It's so inspirational," he told the *Rocky Mountain News* in 2001. "That's what first got me interested in acting. The thought of inspiring other people in the way I've been inspired is amazing." Now that he is in the swing of a major acting career, movies provide an escape. In fact, while on break between *Harry Potter* shoots, Dan likes to lock himself in a small room and just watch films. But don't expect to see him roaring out loud at the latest Will Smith flick or renting a bunch of Bruce Willis action-adventure DVDs. No, just as Dan likes edgy, serious music, his movie taste also reflects a maturity that is beyond his years. He loves the quirky vision of director Wes Anderson and is crazy for his film *The Royal Tenenbaums*. But his favorite film of all time is *12 Angry Men*—a fifties flick starring Henry Fonda, based on a play about jurors trying to decide whether a boy is guilty of murder.

Since he broke in his reading skills on the Harry Potter books, Dan has expanded his literary interests to an eclectic range. He is a huge fan of Douglas Adams and his cult book *The Hitchhiker's Guide to the Galaxy*, which was recently made into a film.

Not all of Dan's pastimes are so sophisticated, however. He is actually a huge fan of World Wrestling Entertainment. It's funny to picture introspective Dan watching men in outlandish getups take each other out in massive smack-downs, but he loves it! Unfortunately, he finds it hard to find time to watch the WWE since he started being Harry Potter, but he told E! Online, "My favorite wrestler is the Rock."

He also has to keep in shape. Dan has a thin frame that looks great on-screen, but to keep fit, he runs a lot and does push-ups. He plays lots of sports with his friends back home, but their favorite is soccer. Football, as it is known in England, is a national obsession.

Although Dan has made millions of dollars, he definitely doesn't go out on shopping sprees. He actually has no idea how much he has earned so far, and he doesn't care either. "I don't need it because I'm just a kid," he told *Time Out*. He did get a serious raise when a British actors' union made a stink that his salary (about $320,000) for the first two films came nowhere near to the astronomical profits the studio was expected to make. He must have been psyched that an organization was helping him with his paycheck. *People* magazine reported that he got a megaraise for his next film—*Prisoner of Azkaban*—for which he earned $3.2 million! But Dan told E! Online, "I'm not doing it for the money. I'm really having fun and meeting wonderful people."

When he is on set, far away from his friends and all the diversions they provide, Dan keeps himself entertained. He maintains his movie addiction with a portable DVD player and loads of films that travel with him wherever he goes. And, of course, he practices the bass guitar that

Gary Oldman gave him. As Dan told the Warner Bros. Web site, "It goes everywhere with me." Who knows, maybe one day Dan will form his own rock group. He told Scholastic Online, "I'd love to play in a band."

13 WHAT'S NEXT

When the inevitable time arrives for Dan and Harry to go their separate ways, Dan's future will be wide open and anything is possible. Who knows what he will try next? He's so talented, not to mention cute, that it's hard to imagine anyone turning him down for any job. One thing is sure: Dan plans on having a life after Harry Potter, whether it's after film five or film seven. And when he gets there, he has a long list of things he would like to do.

Acting is definitely on the list. "I'm incredibly enthusiastic and I love—I love doing it," he told CBS, saying it is definitely a possibility for his future. In the realm of film, he would like to separate himself from the role of Harry Potter, although he knows that reputation will never completely go away. Dan's fine with that. "Harry Potter is such a major achievement that it's not something I want to just forget," he explained.

But acting is only one possibility. From the kid who could hardly make it through a Harry Potter book comes the proclamation that he's considering a life of literature. "I love English, reading, and writing," Dan told *People* in 2002. "I might like to be a writer when I grow up." Or a director. Or a musician. He would also love to make a record one day. There's one thing, however, you will probably never see: Prime Minister Dan Radcliffe. As he told IGN FilmForce, "God help the nation if I'm a politician."

No matter what Dan goes on to do with the rest of his life, Harry Potter will always be a big part of him. He's grateful to be associated with that funny wizard kid, not because the character has earned him millions or garnered him the attention of a thousand screaming babes, but because Harry is a constant reminder that even in real life, anything is possible. "Other than that he's a wizard, he's a really normal person," Dan told the *Philadelphia Inquirer*. "He goes from a zero to a hero, proving that you can do anything."

14 THE BASICS

So you've watched Dan in all the Harry Potter films, read all about him in star magazines and anything else you can get your hands on, hoping to learn everything there is to know about his life, right? Well, here are the important stats you'll need to know in order to become a true Dan Radcliffe expert.

Name: Daniel Jacob Radcliffe

Birthday: July 23, 1989

Birthplace: London, England

Horoscope sign: Leo

Parents: Alan Radcliffe and Marcia Gresham

Hair Color: Dark brown

Eye Color: Blue

Pets: Two dogs, Binka & Nugget

Status: Single

Dan's favorite magic spell: "I'd like to have the invisibility cloak. If you got into trouble, you could just run off really fast," Dan confessed to the *Toronto Sun*. He could also sneak into rock concerts and films without paying, not that Dan really needs to with his four-film paycheck!

Dan's favorite Harry Potter film: *Harry Potter and the Chamber of Secrets*

Dan's favorite Christmas gift: A DVD of *The Royal Tenenbaums*

Dan's favorite book: *Holes* by Louis Sachar and, of course, *Harry Potter and the Chamber of Secrets*.

Dan's favorite wrestler: The Rock

Dan's favorite bands: The Sex Pistols, the New York Dolls, and the Stranglers

Dan's favorite film: *12 Angry Men*

Dan's favorite gadgets: iPods and PlayStation 2

15 FUN FACTS

So now you know all about Dan, but what about the wild world of Harry? There are many Web sites on the Internet devoted to deciphering every little detail of the books and movies. Well, J. K. Rowling wrote a lot of pages, so there is a lot to decipher. But most of us don't have the time or patience to peruse all those sites for hours, days, weeks . . . you get the idea. Don't worry. Here are some of the most fun and interesting Harry Potter trivia you will ever want to know.

Although Harry Potter needs glasses, Dan doesn't. So in all the movies, he wears eyeglasses with plain glass in them that is specially coated not to reflect movie lights.

Peeves the Poltergeist (played by British comedian Rik Mayall), the annoying ghost who likes to pull on Hogwarts students' noses while shouting, "Got your conk!" was actually part of the first Harry Potter film. But he never made it onto the big screen, ending instead on the editing-room floor, since director Chris Columbus didn't like the Peeves design.

In the Harry Potter books, the exact placement of Harry's lightning-bolt scar is never mentioned. On the book covers in the U.S. and England, the illustration showed it in the middle of his forehead. On the big screen it moved to above Harry's right eyebrow. That's because Chris consulted J. K. Rowling. As he told the *Toronto Sun*, he drew a smiley face with a wizard hat and said to her, "Just put the scar on this face and I'll put it on Dan."

Celebrities Kelly Preston and Colin Firth visited the set

of *Chamber of Secrets* on the day before it wrapped shooting. Why? Because they were shooting the comedy *What a Girl Wants* nearby, and who wouldn't want to get a sneak peek at the next Potter flick?

Dan believes in magic, and not just the movie kind. "I've always believed in magic, a hundred percent," he told E! Online. "I'm fascinated by it."

Robbie Coltrane, otherwise known as Hagrid, worked as director Martin Scorsese's driver before he became an actor. When he landed the role in *Harry Potter*, he asked J. K. how he should play the giant. According to E! Online, J. K. told him, "Think of Hagrid as a big Hell's Angel who gets off his bike and tells you how his garden is doing."

J. K. Rowling and Harry Potter share the same birthday: July 31.

In June 2003 Donald Parfitt, a British forklift driver, was sentenced to 180 hours of community service after he stole pages of the *Harry Potter and the Order of the Phoenix* script and tried to sell them to national newspapers.

It costs $740 to hire a Potter impersonator from the U.K.-based A-List Lookalikes & Entertainments Ltd. for four hours.

J. K. Rowling has already written the final chapter of her seventh Harry Potter book and confirmed the last word in the book and the entire series will be "scar."

16 DAN'S DISCOGRAPHY

If you haven't realized it by now, Dan is a huge music fan. "I try my hardest to get as many people into rock music as possible," Dan told BBC's Radio 1. "That's kind of my mission on each film." He's done pretty well at it. He introduced Rupert to a band, the Kings of Leon. Emma has proved to be a more difficult pupil, however. "Emma's taste in music differs greatly from mine," Dan diplomatically told Radio 1. He did manage to get her into one band he loves, Jet. Of course his obsession isn't all about the music. He has a ton of crushes on the leading ladies of rock. He admitted to Radio 1 that he is a sucker for Brody Dalle, the lead singer of the punk band the Distillers, who sports enormous tattoos and thick black eyeliner. "I'm madly in love with her!" Dan said. He also professed love to Marcie Bolen, the adorable redhead guitarist for another punk band, the Von Bondies.

Whenever Dan gets a chance in his superbusy schedule, he'll catch a show. He's been to see the Red Hot Chili Peppers with the Pixies in London's Hyde Park, but his first concert ever was the Strokes. The Pixies, the Von Bondies, the Sex Pistols . . . if you have never heard of any of these names before, don't worry. Below is a little history on some of Dan's favorite bands, so that you can get started on becoming a hardcore rock fan just like him.

The Sex Pistols: This band started in the late seventies when guitarist Steve Jones and drummer Paul Cook met vocalist John Lydon—later known as Johnny Rotten—at a shop owned by their manager. The band's in-your-face music often got them in trouble. Their first single, "Anarchy in the U.K." got the band dropped from their record label. Sid Vicious joined the band as the bassist, although at first he couldn't play his instrument. Even though the Sex Pistols only lasted a couple of years, they changed the history of popular music forever. Their brash sound and raw subjects inspired a massive movement in underground and independent music.

The New York Dolls: This group of guys with big hair, which established itself in 1971, is credited with creating punk rock before the industry even came up with that genre. Their loud music seemed to be the parent of two very unruly children named punk rock and heavy metal. Like the Sex Pistols, the New York Dolls didn't last long. In fact, guitarists Johnny Thunders and Rick Rivets (later replaced by Syl Sylvain), bassist Arthur Kane, drummer Billy Murcia, and vocalist David Johansen only made two studio albums after coming together, but those records influenced a whole generation of musicians.

The Undertones: This punk-pop band came together in Derry, Northern Ireland, in 1976. Guitarists John and Damian O'Neill, bassist Michael Bradley, drummer

Billy Doherty, and lead singer Feargal Sharkey had their breakout hit "Teenage Kicks" in 1978. Their infectious music paid homage to all the ups and downs of adolescence. The band returned in 1983 after a hiatus with *The Sin of Pride*, an album that had a sixties sound to it, but the album didn't rocket to the top of the charts and the Undertones split up.

The Stranglers: Yet another seventies band, this group started out in 1974 as the Guildford Stranglers in England. Once they shortened their name, they quickly broke out of the small pub circuit they had been playing to perform in much bigger venues. Their music related much of the alienation and anger that was typical of this early punk movement. Despite all the controversy surrounding the band's reputation as a bunch of bad boys, their music, including "Peaches" and "Something Better Change," had a hold on the charts. They continued to record music into the early nineties, but their early years remain their most popular.

The Pixies: Although the members of the Pixies weren't

accomplished musicians when they began, their band was one of the most influential in the American alternative rock scene of the late eighties. The combination of melodic pop, mysterious lyrics, and heavy guitar licks quickly put them on every indie rocker's listening list. The Pixies formed in Boston in 1986 when roommates Charles Thompson and Joey Santiago found bassist/vocalist Kim Deal by taking out an ad in a music trade paper. Kim found them drummer David Lovering. They recorded eighteen songs in just three days in 1987, which eventually got them signed to a record label. They went on to become a worldwide sensation, but rock radio never put their singles into regular rotation. Eventually tensions among band mates broke up the group in the early nineties.